The Aussie Bible

(Well, bits of it anyway!)

Re-told by Kel Richards
Bible Society NSW
Produced by Glencroix Promotions, Inc.

The Aussie Bible (Well, bits of it anyway!)
by Kel Richards

Originally published by Bible Society NSW
5 Byfield Street, Macquarie Park, NSW 2113
Australia
August 2003

Text:
© Bible Society NSW

US Edition:
Re-printed with exclusive permission by Glencroix Promotions, Inc.
Philadelphia, Pennsylvania 19130
USA
July 2004

Exclusive License to reprint and distribute *The Aussie Bible*
(Well, bits of it anyway!) for US rights to hardback, paperback
and audio books granted to Glencroix Promotions, Inc.
(Philadelphia, Pennsylvania: July 2004 renewable through July 2014).

Layout and graphic design:
www.madebydesign.net

ISBN: 0 647 50848 6
Printed in USA 2004

www.theaussiebible.com

GLENCROIX

Contents

Press Release

28th May 2004

Beaudy, bottler, ripper mate!
Aussie Bible hits '100,000 mark'

'The Aussie Bible (Well, bits of it anyway!)' written by Kel Richards and published by Bible Society NSW has reached the 100,000 mark. Released in August 2003, the story of the life of Jesus told in 'old bush vernacular' has been an outstanding success, said Bible Society NSW Communication Manager, Martin Johnson.

"The acceptance of the book by Christians and non-Christians alike has been remarkable," said Martin. "Every day we hear stories of how people are using the book to introduce their non-Christians friends to the person of Jesus Christ."

Author Kel Richards, who has published over 28 books said "Well, stone the crows! Who'da thought it? It's good news that so many Aussies want to read good news. And some of them might go further, and join the Jesus fan club. That wouldn't be a bad thing for the land-down-under, now would it? Be better than a poke in the eye with a burnt stick!"

Kel – a well known ABC broadcaster and journalist – took the story of Jesus' life from the New Testament and re-told it in chronological order using the Aussie idiom. Familiar characters and stories such as the 'good samaritan' become the story of 'a good bloke', with the feeding of the five thousand called 'a gigantic picnic'.

Glencroix Promotions, Inc. with permission from Bible Society NSW has also released *The Aussie Bible* on CD courtesy of Anglican Media. Both products are available from Glencroix Promotions, Inc. at your local bookstore or on the net at www.theaussiebible.com

Introduction

by Dr Peter Jensen
Archbishop of Sydney

As migrants tell us, even if we learn our new language well, we don't always use it. When we speak intimately to our family, or to our God, we prefer to use the language of our heart, our mother tongue.

When many people first become Christian they don't have the Bible in their own language. They read it in another language, if at all. I am told that it is a very emotional moment when you can begin to read God's word for yourself in the language of your heart.

Of course the Bible has been in English for a long time. But Kel Richards has given us an Aussie Bible and, when I read it, I was surprised by my own feelings. It is not a translation. It is more like a re-telling of what it would be like if the whole story had happened here, and been written down in our sort of style.

I hope that you can feel the impact of it. I hope that you can begin to see that the events of the Bible happened to real people in a real place, not so very different from our people and our place.

In particular, I hope that reading this book will help you to see Jesus and learn to trust him from the heart.

—Peter Jensen

The Gospel Story

The intro *(Luke 1:1-4)*

G'day.

Lots of other blokes have had a go at telling you what happened—sticking to the ridgy didge, fair dinkum facts, having got the good oil straight from the horse's mouth. And I've had a yarn with a whole lot of the blokes that were there and saw it all—and heard it—so I thought I'd have a go too at sorting it all out, and making it clear, so that you'll know, Theo old mate, that you're not being a mug, but you've got it straight.

Surprising news *(Luke 1:5-25)*

In the days when old Herod was boss cocky of Judea there was a sky pilot called Zechariah (known to his mates as "Zeck"), who was married to a sheila named Libby. They were both good, decent sort of people who'd lend you a cup of sugar or a fiver till payday. But they had no ankle biters, because poor Lib had this medical problem, on top of which they were both getting a bit wrinkly.

Anyway, one time when Zeck was on duty at the Temple in Jerusalem, they drew straws to see who'd go into the inner room to light the candles, and Zeck got the short straw.

When it was lighting up time everyone was hanging around outside, praying and so on, and Zeck barged in and got the fright of his life—right in front of him was an angel, as large as life and twice as ugly.

Zeck turned as white as a sheet, but the angel said, "Pull yourself together old son. Your prayers have been heard. You and Libby will have a kid—and you have to name the little sprog John. He'll be a really cute little tyke who'll brighten up your life, and there'll be more than just you and Lib who'll end up being glad he was born. That's because God's got his eye on your John. He'll be a teetotaller, who'll know what God wants, and will nag away at the conscience of the nation. Lots of blokes will turn back to God because of him. You've read the yarns about Elijah, back in the olden days—well, it'll be the same stuff all over again with your John."

Zeck shook his head and said, "Come off the grass. How can we have a kid? Me and Libby are old codgers."

The angel said, "Listen, mate: I am Gabriel, you've heard of me, right? Well, I've come from God with this bit of good news for you, and all you do is whinge! So, from now on your mouth is as dumb as your brain—all because you wouldn't believe what you were told,"

Meanwhile, the crowd outside was wondering

what had happened to Zeck—it doesn't take all that long to light the candles, so what was he up to?

When Zeck finally came out, he couldn't speak. "What's up?" they all said, "Cat got your tongue?" They worked out something pretty stunning had happened, because he kept waving his hands about trying to make them understand.

When his time on the roster was up, he went back home.

And sure enough, not long afterwards, Libby was preggers—definitely had a bun in the oven. For the first five months of the pregnancy she kept herself pretty much to herself. "This is God's doing," she said. "He's seen to it that I can become a mum, just like all of my girlfriends."

A message for Mary (Luke 1:26-38)

When Libby was six months gone, God sent the same angel—this Gabriel bloke—to a backblocks town called Nazareth, in Galilee shire, to a nice young girl who was engaged to the local carpenter, Joe Davidson. Her name was Mary.

The angel said to her, "G'day Mary. You are a pretty special sheila. God has his eye on you."

Mary went weak at the knees, and wondered what was going on.

But the angel said to her, "Don't panic, don't chuck a wobbly. God thinks you're okay. You're about to become pregnant, and you'll have a son, and you're to call him Jesus. He will be a very big wheel, and will be called the Son of God Most High.

God will give him the throne of his father—your ancestor—King David, and he will be in charge of the whole show forever."

"But how?" said Mary. "Joe and I have done the right thing, we've never... well, you know. I mean to say, I'm still a virgin."

The angel answered, "Leave the mechanics up to God. This is heavenly stuff. God's Spirit will come upon you, and the Big Brain behind the Big Bang will manipulate the necessary molecules to make it happen. So this little kid of yours will be as special as it's possible to be, and he'll be called God's own Son. Look, even Libby, your old cousin, is preggers—at her age! God can do these things. In fact, Libby is in her sixth month because nothing is impossible with God."

"God's in charge," Mary answered. "If that's what God wants, then it's what I want."

Then the angel nicked off and left her alone.

Mary visits Elizabeth (Luke 1:39-56)

Mary didn't muck about. She got packed and ankled it up to a town in the hills, where she went straight to Zeck and Libby's place, so that she could say "G'day" to Lib. When Libby heard Mary's "Cooee" at the front door the baby in her womb gave a kick like a footie player at a grand final, and Lib was filled with God's Spirit. With a big grin, and a voice that could rattle windows, she said: "Good onya Mary! You beaut! God's chosen you out of all the sheilas in the world, and your baby will be God's toddler. But, stone the crows, why would the mum of my Big Boss, my Lord, come and see me? As soon as I heard the sound of your voice my little bun in the oven went bananas with excitement. Good onya for believing what God told you—for believing that God can do what he says he can do."

And then Mary said, "My soul is as happy as Larry with God and my mind is just buzzing with God my Rescuer because he picked me—me! And I'm about as important as a bottle washer's assistant! But from now on everyone who ever lives will call me well off—looked after by God—for the One who can do anything has done great things for me. His name is the only Name that matters. His gentleness rolls on like a river. He has done great things that would just knock your socks off. The rich, the stuffed shirts, the boss cockies, don't impress God; he knocks them off their perch. But those who don't have tickets on themselves he gives a hand to. He provides tucker for the hungry and sends the toffee noses away without a feed. He has wrapped his great arms around his chosen. He hasn't forgotten his kindness and gentleness. Exactly what he promised yonks ago is what is happening now."

Mary stayed with Libby for a few months and then nicked off back home again.

John is born (Luke 1:57-66)

When her nine months were up Libby popped her sprog. The next-door neighbours and the rellies all heard that God had been kind to her, and were tickled pink.

On the eighth day they came to circumcise the little tyke (as the habit was in those days) and they were going to call him "Zeck" after his Dad, but his mum spoke up and said, "Not on your Nellie. Call him 'John'."

They said, "But hang on—you haven't got any rels named 'John'."

They made signs to Zeck, his Dad, to find out what handle he wanted to give the kid. He asked for a bit of paper and pencil, and he knocked them all for six when he scribbled down, "His name is 'John'." At once Zeck could talk again, and then he couldn't stop yabbering, saying how terrific God was. The next-door neighbours had the wind knocked right out of them by this, and soon the bush telegraph was full of it, and in the hill country it was all they talked about.

Zeck has a few words to say *(Luke 1:67-80)*

John's Dad, Zeck, was full of God's Spirit, and said: "Good on God, the Lord, the Boss, the God of his people, because he's begun his rescue mission to Planet Earth. He is flying the flag of old King David as he promised yonks and yonks ago. His cavalry is riding to our rescue. He'll rescue us from the sharks who run this world and we'll be his, and we'll be free to follow his orders without a care in the world. And you, my son, will be the mouthpiece of the Maker. You'll go first to get things ready, to tell people the Rescuer and Ruler is on his way so they can have their slates wiped clean. God's sunshine is about to pop through the clouds and send the shadows scooting away showing us the track through the bush—the path of peace."

And the kiddie grew up, until he was as big as a full back and as strong as a Mallee bull, and he lived out in the bush—all alone like a bandicoot on a burnt ridge—until it was time for him to start spreading the news.

Jesus is born (Luke 2:1-7)

In those days Caesar Augustus ordered a head count of the whole Roman world. (This was the first big tally, when Quirinius ran the Syrian branch of the empire.) And everyone had to go back to the bit of country they were born in to fill in the forms.

So Joe hiked up from Nazareth (in Galilee shire) to Bethlehem (in Judea shire) because this spot in the mulga was where King David came from, and Joe's family tree had King David up in the top branches. He went there to fill in the forms and sign the register with his fiancée, Mary, who was pretty near nine months by this time. While they were there, she gave birth to a baby boy. She wrapped him in a bunny rug, and tucked him up in a feed trough in a back shed, because the pub was full to bursting.

News flash (Luke 2:8-21)

There were some drovers, camped out in a paddock nearby, keeping an eye on their mob of sheep that night. Their eyes shot out on stalks when an angel of the Lord zapped into view, and the glory of the Lord filled the air like a thousand volts of electricity. The angel said: "Stop looking like a bunch of stunned mullets. Let me give you the drum, the good oil, it's top news for the whole crew—everyone, everywhere. Today in that little town on the hill a rescuer has been born: he is the Promised One, the King, the Lord. And here's how you'll find him: the little nipper is wrapped up in a bunny rug, and lying in a food trough."

And before you could say, "Well, I'll be blowed!" the whole sky was filled with more angels than you could count, all singing away at the top of their lungs (if angels have got lungs, that is): "God is great! God is bonzer—and to everyone on this planet who's on God's side: peace and goodwill, and, by the way, Happy Christmas."

(Which rather confused the drovers because they'd never heard of Christmas before.)

Suddenly the whole choir had nipped off in the blink of an eye. The drovers said to each other, "We'd better make tracks to Bethlehem and have a squiz at what's happened—check out this message from God."

So the lot of them shot through like a Toorak tram to Bethlehem—and they found Mary, and Joe and the baby who was, sure enough, wrapped in a bunny rug and lying in a food trough. When they'd seen this they told every Tom, Dick and Harry about what had happened, and everyone who heard the story was blown away by it. But Mary just made a mental note of these things, and tucked them away in a corner of her heart. The drovers went back to the paddock, and their mob of sheep, as excited as a race horse on Melbourne Cup day, and saying what a bottler God was, because everything was spot on—just as they'd been told.

Simeon (Luke 2:22-35)

On the eighth day, at his circumcision, Joe and Mary's little kid was given the name Jesus—the name the angel gave him when he turned up with the big announcement.

When all the bits and pieces required by the old laws had been done, Joe and Mary took their baby to Jerusalem to say "Thank you" to God, and to say "He's yours." (Because God's Book says: "If a woman's first baby is a boy, he's to be dedicated to God") and to make an offering of a couple of budgies, as required by the old law.

Now there was an old codger in Jerusalem named Simeon who was a dead-set good bloke. He was waiting for the coming of the king God had promised yonks ago. God's Spirit had given him the nod that he wouldn't tumble off the twig until he'd seen him. And God's Spirit gave him the whisper that he should go to the Temple that day, so, when Mary and Joe arrived with their baby, Jesus, Simeon was there. He said, "Can I have a nurse of the bub?" And as he took him in his arms he said, "Dear God, now I can die a happy bloke—I have seen the Promised One, just as you said I would. I have seen the One who is your Rescue Mission to the world. He will be a lighthouse—a spotlight—and by this light people from all over the shop will see how terrific you are."

The baby's Mum and Dad were staggered by this. Then old Simeon said, "God bless you all," and he said to Mary, "This boy will be good news to heaps of people and bad news to heaps of others. Many won't like him, and will put the boot in. And he will show up many of them for what they are. And your own heart will be broken one day, too."

Anna *(Luke 2:36-38)*

There was also at the Temple an old duck named Anna. Her Dad had been a bloke named Phanuel Asher. She'd been married for seven years, and then her old man had carked it, and since then she'd been a widow. She was now 84. She was a real devout old duck, always up at the Temple. She too came up to Mary and Joe, just to say thanks to God, and tell everyone who was waiting for the Promised One that he had turned up.

The wise guys *(Matthew 2:1-12)*

When Jesus was born in the township of Bethlehem, in Judea shire (when Herod was the kingpin) some egg-heads from out east turned up in Jerusalem asking everyone: "Where's this new Prince of the Jews, this Promised One, who's just been born? We saw his star out east, and we've come to say 'G'day Your Majesty'."

Now this made Herod as jumpy as a wallaby on hot rocks, and stirred up the whole town. So Herod got some of his cronies together—smart blokes who had more degrees than a thermometer—and asked them where the Promised One was supposed to be born.

They said Bethlehem was the spot, and quoted the words of the prophet:

> Bethlehem is a little place
> But landing here from outer space
> Will be a Leader who will keep
> A shepherd's eye on all the sheep.

So Herod called the eastern egg-heads to a secret meeting and asked them when the star had first popped up. Then he told them to nick off to Bethlehem, search around the township, and find this kid.

"When you find him," said Herod, "send me the word and I'll pop across and have a squiz at him too."

After the king had earbashed them they took off for Bethlehem. The star they'd seen out east was there, and they were beside themselves. They hurried into the cottage and found the baby, with Mary his Mum, and they bowed and scraped and gave him some terrific pressies: gold and frankincense and myrrh (strange pressies for a baby, but better than a hankie or a pair of socks).

In a dream God told them to avoid Herod like the plague, so they set off back home, taking a different road.

Escape! (Matthew 2:13-15)

Then Joe had a dream, in which he saw God's angel saying: "Hop up! Take the baby and his Mum and make tracks for Egypt quick smart! Stay there till I give you the nod, because Herod is going bananas over this."

Even though it was the middle of the night, Joe bundled them up and set off for Egypt in two ticks. They stayed there until Herod was safely dead, fulfilling the old prediction: "I called my Son out of Egypt."

Slaughter! (Matthew 2:16-18)

When Herod discovered the eastern egg-heads had diddled him he turned very nasty. He sent his thugs to the Bethlehem district to kill all the little boys under two (based on what the egg-heads had said).

This fulfilled Jeremiah's prediction:

> *A weeping voice will wail and mourn*
> *For the babies who were born*
> *"There is no comfort," they all cried,*
> *"For all the Mums whose babies died."*

Home again (Matthew 2:19-23)

With Herod himself dead God's angel once again spoke to Joe (in Egypt) in a dream and said: "It's okay to take the baby and his Mum back to Israel, because that nasty piece of work is now pushing up daisies."

Joe and his little family set off for Israel. But when he heard that Herod's son Archelaus had seized power in Judea he knew that only a dill would go there. And after getting another dream message from God headed off for Galilee, and set up home in the township of Nazareth. This was another prediction fulfilled: "He will be called a Nazarene."

Snapshot of Jesus: aged 12 *(Luke 2:41-52)*

Every year Joe and Mary went up to Jerusalem for a big do called Passover Day. When Jesus was 12 he went with them—like most 12-year-olds. After the festivities were over, while his Mum and Dad were on their way back home, young Jesus stayed behind in Jerusalem, but because the road was chockers he wasn't missed. Thinking he was somewhere with the Nazareth mob they hiked on all day. Then, blow me down, when they looked: he wasn't there! When none of their friends, and none of their rels, had seen him, they headed back to the Big Smoke. For three days they frantically hunted in every nook and cranny, and finally found him in the Temple, with the Teachers, the big wigs, listening and asking questions. When his Mum and Dad saw where he was they were knocked sideways. His Mum said, "We've been worried silly about you. Your Dad and I have searched all over the place for you."

"Why search?" Jesus replied, "Hadn't you tumbled to the fact that I'd be here in the Temple, my Father's House?" But his Mum and Dad just scratched their heads—they hadn't a clue what he meant.

Then it was back to Nazareth, where Jesus was a good son to them. Mary tucked these little memories away in a corner of her heart. Jesus grew up to be sensible and smart, and tall and strong. And everyone liked him—the blokes around him, and God too.

John the Baptist *(Luke 3:1-20)*

This brings us to some 15 years after Tiberius Caesar took over running the whole Roman Mob. A bloke named Pontius Pilate had the franchise for Judea, while Herod ran Galilee shire, his brother Phil ran the Iturea and Trachonitis branch, and Lysanias controlled Abilene. Two blokes named Annas and Caiaphas ran things at the Temple.

God gave the whisper to John (the son of Zeck) in his desert humpy. So John went all over the Jordan water catchment area calling on everyone to turn back to God to get their slate wiped clean. This is what old Isaiah said yonks ago: "a voice, shouting from the bush, 'Prepare a track for the Lord to travel on. Widen the track, spread out the gravel, cut down the bumps, fill up the dips, straighten the curves, smooth out the ruts—and everyone'll see the arrival of God's Rescue Mission to Planet Earth.'"

Here's a sample of John's preaching to the crowds that came out to be baptised by him: "You mob of snakes! God's very aggro with you! Who warned you to try to scuttle out of the way? Don't just say, 'Abraham was our old man.' God can make kids for Abraham out of lumps of rock if he wants to! God's axe is already hanging over your heads, and you'll be cut down unless you turn over a new leaf."

"This is a tall order," the mob whinged. "If God stacks on a turn, what can we do?"

"If you've got a couple of coats," said John, "give one to a bloke who's freezing. Share your tucker with folks that need a feed."

Even the tax collectors—who were sharks and bushrangers—came along and said, "What do you want us to do?"

John said, "Give people a square deal. Stop robbing them blind."

And some soldiers said, "What about us?"

John said, "Don't behave like thugs. Don't demand money with menaces. Just live on your pay packet."

Everyone got real excited and said, "Could John be the Promised One?"

But John said, "Look, I'm just baptising with water. But another bloke is coming, who runs on six cylinders compared to my one. I'm not good enough to put his thongs on his feet. He'll baptise not with water, but fire—and with God's Spirit. He's ready to drive his harvester over the paddock: the grain goes into the silo, but the chaff is chucked out and burned—in the fire that never goes out."

That's how John told the people the Good News.

But John also ticked off Herod, boss of Galilee, because of a bird called Herodias (his brother Phil's wife) and a stack of other stuff he'd done wrong. Naturally Herod stacked on a turn, and chucked John in prison—making one more wrong thing he'd done.

Jesus gets baptised *(Luke 3:21-22)*

When the crowds were being baptised, Jesus joined the queue, and he too was baptised. Then, as he prayed, the sky opened up and God's Spirit came down, like a big white cockatoo, and settled on him. God said: "You are my own dear Son, and I'm really pleased with you."

A battle of wills (Matthew 4:1-11)

God's Spirit led Jesus away from the river beyond the driest part of the bush to the stony desert where Old Nick nagged at him for 40 days. During that whole time Jesus didn't have a bite to eat, and by the end his stomach thought his throat had been cut.

Then that old devil said to him, "If you're God's Son, use your powers to turn this lump of rock into a nice piece of fresh damper."

Jesus answered: "The Bible says you can't live on just tucker—to survive you need every word God has spoken."

Then Old Nick whipped him up to the top of the Temple tower, and said: "You can easily impress this little lot. Show them you're God's own Son—jump off! There's a bit in your precious Bible that says, 'God will send his angels to stop you splattering like tomato sauce on the footpath.'"

Jesus answered: "The Bible also says, 'Don't think up foolish tests for God, your Lord.'"

Finally, Old Nick took him to a hilltop and pointed out all the kingdoms of the world, saying, "The whole lot can be yours, Jesus my lad. You can have the whole lot bowing and scraping to you—at a perfectly reasonable price. Just bow down to me, and with a snap of my fingers, they're all yours.

Now I can't say fairer than that, can I?"

Jesus answered: "The Bible says that only God is God, and God is the only one we should serve as God."

At this point Old Nick chucked in the towel—at least for the time being.

The work begins (Luke 4:14-15)

Jesus went back to Galilee shire, and pretty soon the bush telegraph was filled with news about him. He gave talks in the Jewish Meeting Halls, and everyone said he was a knockout speaker.

Hometown blues (Luke 4:16-30)

He went back to his hometown of Nazareth, and on Saturday he went to the Jewish Meeting Hall, and stood up to read the Bible. The bit he read came from Isaiah, and he read these words: "God's Spirit is on me. He's picked me to tell good news to the poor, set the prisoners free, open the eyes of the blind, give a hand to the downtrodden, and tell everyone this is the time God has chosen." Then he closed the Bible, gave it back to the usher and sat down. Everyone's eyes were glued on him as he said, "This bit of the Bible has come true today, right here and now."

The whole mob liked him, and spoke well of him, and said how well he spoke. "How come?" they all said, "this is just the carpenter's kid!"

Jesus said to them: "I reckon I know what you're going to say, you'll quote the old proverb, 'Doctor, treat your own illness'—meaning, 'Do the stuff

here, in your hometown, you did in Capernaum.'
But, straight up, no one who speaks God's words
is listened to in his hometown. Back in Elijah's day
there was a drought for three and half years and
everyone was scratching for food. There were heaps
of widows in Israel—but God didn't send Elijah to
any of them, but to a foreign widow (in Zeraphath,
on the Sidon road). And in Elisha's day there were
heaps of lepers in Israel, but the one God healed
was a foreigner—Naaman, the Syrian."

At this the whole mob blew a fuse, and decided
to throw him out of town. Worse, they dragged him
to a cliff and were about to chuck him down, when
they found he'd slipped through their fingers, and
left them.

A tormented man *(Luke 4:31-37)*

Jesus went to Capernaum (also in Galilee shire),
and on a Saturday he began to teach the mob there.
They were staggered because this was clearly a
bloke who knew what he was talking about.

In the Jewish Meeting Hall there was a bloke
with a devil of a spirit in him who yelled out, "Oy,
Jesus of Nazareth! Have you come to do us in? I've
got your number—you're the Promised One of God,
aren't you?"

But Jesus cut off this racket by saying, "Silence!
Leave this bloke and shove off." Then the bloke
fell in a heap, and the devil of a spirit nicked off,
leaving him without a scratch.

This took everyone's breath away. "What is this?"

they all said. "This bloke says 'Jump!' and they say 'How high?' Amazing!" And soon the gossip mills were grinding out this latest news about Jesus.

A crowded surgery *(Luke 4:38-44)*

Jesus left the Jewish Meeting Hall and popped into Peter's place because Pete's mother-in-law was feeling crook, and Jesus had been asked to see what he could do. So Jesus bent over her and ticked off the colly wobbles that had her feeling rotten, and—bingo!—she was better. She got straight up and put on the kettle to make them all a cuppa.

At sundown they started flocking in—it was like a hospital waiting room. Jesus touched each one, and they were okay. And more of those mad demons came out of people, bellowing, "You... you... you are God's own Son!" Jesus gave them their marching orders, and made them stop their babbling, because they knew he was the Promised One.

At the crack of dawn Jesus went out to be on his own. But the mob went hunting for him, because they didn't want him to leave. "I have to," said Jesus. "My job is telling the Good News in other towns too. That's my job." And he kept on speaking in the Jewish Meeting Halls in Judea shire.

Jesus goes "head hunting" *(Luke 5:1-11)*

One day Jesus was down by the water's edge at Lake Gennesaret, with heaps of people crowding round, listening to his message from God. On the shore were a couple of skiffs belonging to the fishermen. Jesus got into the one belonging to Simon, and told him to row out just a little. And then he talked to the mob on the shore from his seat in the back of the boat.

When he'd finished, he turned to Simon and said, "Pull out into the deeper water and drop your nets."

"Fair go!" complained Simon. "We've fished all night and haven't even caught a tiddler. But, okay, if you reckon—well, we'll do it."

This time when they tried to yank the nets back into the boat they almost tore, they were so full. Simon yelled out to his mates to come out in their boat and give him a hand. Soon both boats were so full of fish, and so low in the water, that a good wave might have sunk them.

This shook Simon up no end. He looked up at Jesus and said, "You oughta clear off. I'm not a good bloke." Simon and all his mates were almost speechless at the size of the catch—and so were his partners in the fishing business, Jim and John Zebedee.

"Don't panic," said Jesus. "Calm down. From now on you'll be catching blokes, not fish."

So they rowed to the shore, left their fishing tackle where it was, and followed Jesus.

Leprosy! (Luke 5:12-16)

While Jesus was in a little township, a bloke came up with really bad leprosy. When he saw Jesus he just dropped in the dust, and pleaded with him, "Sir—if you want to, you can heal these sores and make me well and whole."

"I certainly want to," Jesus said, reaching out and touching the leper. Then Jesus gave an order to the man's skin: "Be clean!" In the blink of an eye—no leprosy!

Jesus gave the bloke strict orders: "Don't go blabbing about this, just get yourself off to the Temple, and follow all the rules, so that you can be registered as officially clean and healed."

But the news got out anyway, and the mobs got bigger and bigger—every man and his dog wanted to get an instant cure. But Jesus took off to a quiet spot, so he could pray.

Forgiveness power (Luke 5:17-26)

One day a bunch of lawyers was hanging around listening to Jesus. They'd come from just about every township in Galilee shire, and Judea shire, and from the Big Smoke—from Jerusalem.

God gave Jesus tons of power to heal the sick.

But then, blow me down, some blokes were trying to get their paralysed mate on a stretcher to Jesus, but it was like a Grand Final crowd that day and they couldn't barge through. So they dragged their mate on the stretcher up onto the roof, yanked off a few tiles, and then lowered him down smack in the middle of the room.

When Jesus saw how much trust in him there was, he said to the paralysed bloke, "Old chap, your sins are forgiven."

The lawyers sneered, "This boofhead thinks he's God! Only God can forgive sins!"

But Jesus knew what was going on inside their noggins, and he said to them, "So, that's what you think, is it? Just watch this. Which of these is easier: to say to this bloke 'Your sins are forgiven'? or to say to him 'You're cured, get up and walk'? Now this ought to show you that I have the power to forgive sins." He turned to the paralysed bloke and said, "Hop up, pick up your stretcher, and go home."

Straight off, the bloke stood up, and picked up his stretcher. The crowd parted in front of him like the Red Sea in front of Moses, and he set off for his home, saying how terrific God was! Everyone was staggered and said, "Well! Starve the lizards! How about that!"

An unlikely team member (Luke 5:27-32)

A bit later Jesus came across a local bloke who collected taxes for the Roman army—a bloke called Matt Levi—sitting at his desk, and Jesus said to him, "Follow me." The taxman left his account books (and the cash drawer!) and followed Jesus.

Then Matt Levi turned on a humdinger of a barbie on his front veranda, and all his mates from the tax office were there, getting stuck into the snags and tomato sauce along with Jesus and his mates.

So the lawyers got all snide again and yelled out, "Why are you hanging around with that bunch of sharks?"

Jesus said, "Blokes who are in the pink don't need a doctor, only those who are crook. I've come to call the wrong 'uns to turn away from their wrongdoing and turn back to God. I haven't come for the blokes who think they're already hunky dory."

Skipping meals (Luke 5:33-39)

Their next big whinge was that Jesus and his mates were feasting, not fasting. And they said, "Zeck's son John—who did all that baptising in the river— he and his mates used to pray instead of eat, while your lot are forever putting on the billy or dipping into the tucker bag."

Jesus told them, "It's like a wedding. What do you do at a wedding? Do you starve, or do you get stuck into the grub? Time's coming when I'll be taken away from them, then they won't feel like eating."

Then Jesus said, "Look, it's like this. No one patches up an old pair of jeans with a bit of new, unshrunk denim. When it starts to shrink it'll just tear off and make an even worse hole. And no one puts that latest wine harvest into old barrels that are dried up and cracked—the barrels would burst and you'd lose the lot. New wine goes in new barrels. Of course, after drinking the vintage stuff, no one wants the new wine. 'Let it age,' they say, 'the old is the best.'"

A proper day off (Luke 6:1-5)

On one particular day off (a Saturday in that part of the world) Jesus and his mates were walking through a wheat paddock. Some of the blokes pulled off a couple of ears of wheat, and rubbed them in their hands (the way you do, to get the husks off) and ate the wheat.

At this some of the lawyers did their lolly. "Oy," they said, "that's illegal. You're not allowed to work on a day off, that's our law, and harvesting wheat is work."

Jesus replied, "Haven't you read your Bibles? Haven't you read what King David did when his men were hungry? He went into the Temple and nicked the holy bread that was supposed to be for the priests. He not only ate some himself, he gave it to his men too." Then he added, "I am Master even of Days Off (in your case, that means Saturdays)."

A bloke with a crippled hand *(Luke 6:6-11)*

On another day off (another Saturday) when Jesus went to the Jewish Meeting Hall to give a talk, there was a bloke there whose hand was all withered up. The lawyers were watching Jesus like a hawk to see if he'd have a go at healing on a day off. But Jesus knew what was ticking over inside their heads, so he told the bloke with the crook hand to stand up where everyone could have a good squiz at him.

Then Jesus turned to the lawyers and said, "Okay then, what will the law let you do on a day off—hurt or help? To make someone's life better or worse?"

After he looked everyone straight in the eye, Jesus said to the bloke, "Stretch out your crook hand." He did, and, of course, it wasn't crook anymore—it was perfectly okay.

At this the lawyers were as mad as a cut snake with Jesus, muttering, "We've got to do something about this bloke."

Jesus picks his team (Luke 6:12-16)

Jesus used to nick off up to the high country to pray. He prayed all night long, and then in the morning he called his mates together. From them he chose the twelve, to be the leaders. He picked Simon (and nicknamed him "Peter"); his brother Andy; another pair of brothers, Jim and John; and Phil; and Bart; and Matt; and Tom; another Jim (whose old man was named Alf); another Simon (this bloke used to belong to the People's Democratic Action Front); and Judas (whose Dad was an old bloke named Jim); and Judas Iscariot—the snake in the grass.

On the road (Luke 6:17-19)

Jesus and his chosen team leaders, the twelve, came down to the lower slopes. He was joined there by heaps of his other mates and a huge mob of people from all over the shop—from Judea shire, and Jerusalem, and the beach resorts of Tyre and Sidon. Heaps of them were as sick as dogs and came to be healed—which they were. Some had really bad spirits, and these got fixed too. Everyone just wanted to touch him, because when they did it was like high voltage power shot out of him and into them and they were healed.

The master class begins (Luke 6:20-26)

Jesus said to his mates: "You're well off if you're poor—because God's kingdom is yours. You're well off if you're hungry—because later you'll be satisfied. You're well off if your heart's broken now—because later you'll smile. You're well off when blokes hate you, and turn their backs on you, and make fun of you, because of me. You ought to be pleased when that happens, tickled pink in fact, because your pay off is stacked up in heaven. The prophets, back in the old days, got the same treatment.

"But look out if you're rich—you've got all your goodies now, so there's nothing good coming for you. Look out if you're fat and well fed now—there's starvation in your future. Look out when everyone and his dog says what a top bloke you are—that's how they used to go on about the prophets who told lies back in the old days (so what does that say about you, eh?)"

Play straight (Luke 6:27-38)

Jesus said: "This is the good word for anyone who'll bother to listen. Be a good mate even to blokes who are rotten to you, be a cobber even if they stab you in the back. If someone gives you curry, be nice to them. Ask God to be nice to someone who gives you heaps. If someone wallops you, let 'em do it again. If someone wants your jacket, give 'em the shirt off your back too. Put your hand in your pocket for everyone who wants a hand out. If someone takes all your stuff, don't get cheesed off and ask for it back. Treat everyone like a mate—the way you'd like a mate to treat you.

"If you're only a mate to those who are a mate to you, what's the big deal in that? Even cadgers and touts do that! You don't win brownie points with trade-offs, like 'I'll scratch your back if you scratch mine'. If you lend someone a quid just so they'll buy you a beer, what's so great about that? Even a tea-leaf'll lend a quid to another tea-leaf, if he thinks there's something in it for him. Be a real cobber to everyone, even the crooks and whingers, and open your wallet even for the dead beats. Then you'll be showing a sort of 'family resemblance' to God, and there's a pay off in that. Be open-handed, just like God's open-handed."

Jesus said: "Don't go around running people down, or the same thing'll happen to you. Forgive and forget when someone messes you about—then God will forgive and forget when you mess him about. Don't be stingey with anything you do for others—because these things boomerang."

Paint me a picture! (Luke 6:39-49)

Jesus also used some word pictures. He said: "Picture one blind bloke leading another. They'll both wind up down the bottom of a gully. An apprentice is not better than a tradesman, but if he pays attention he'll end up as a tradesman himself.

"How come you can spot a speck of dust in a mate's eye and miss a telegraph pole in your own eye? How come you'll say, 'Hey, mate, let me get that speck of dust out of your eye,' when you've got a dirty great telegraph pole or railway sleeper in your own? Come off it! First take the lump out of your own eye, then you'll be able to see to take the speck out of your mate's eye.

"Rotten fruit doesn't grow on decent trees. You don't pick apples off orange trees, or blackberries off grape vines. A decent bloke's okay because his heart's in the right place. But a snake in the grass has a scheming heart. What a bloke says, and does, and thinks, shows what's really going on in his heart. What's the point of calling me 'boss' or 'chief' if you don't follow my orders?"

The bright bloke and the boofhead (Matthew 7:24-27)

Jesus said: "Everyone who lends an ear to what I say, and then puts it into practice (turns around and changes how they live) is like a smart bloke who built his homestead on a good foundation of rock. A cyclone hit that could blow the thoughts right out of your head. It was a lazy wind—wouldn't blow round you, blew straight through you. But wind, rain, whatever, that house on the rock foundations was safe.

"But everyone who lends an ear to what I say, and then doesn't put it into practice (just goes on like they've always done) is like a real boofhead who built his homestead on a foundation of sand! Same cyclone hit, and there wasn't one board left nailed to another when the wind and rain was over. They were picking up bits of it in Broome. That homestead was a real goner."

Jesus' authority is recognised *(Luke 7:1-10)*

When he knocked off from this teaching session
Jesus went into Capernaum. There he met an army
Major who had a servant who was real crook—one
foot in the grave. So the Major asked some of the
leading Jews to have a word with Jesus, and ask him
to heal the servant.

They said, "Please help him. This Major is a
decent sort. He's been a mate to us, and built our
meeting house for us."

So Jesus went with them. But when he was
within spitting distance of the house the Major sent
someone out to say, "Sir, I shouldn't be mucking you
about like this. I'm not worth all this trouble. That's
why I didn't come myself, and why you shouldn't
come to my house. You just give the order—just say
the word—and my bloke will be okay. I'm in the
army, I know what it's like. When I give an order
to one of my soldiers he snaps to attention, salutes,
and does it."

Jesus heard these words and was pretty
impressed. "All over the shop," he said, "I've never
found anyone who trusted me like this."

The Major's mates went back to his house and
found the servant fit as a fiddle.

Cancel that death certificate! *(Luke 7:11-17)*

Soon Jesus and his followers were on the road to
the township of Nain, and a whole mob tagged
along with them. On the outskirts of the town they
came across a funeral procession. The dead man was

his widowed mum's only son. She was there, and half the town was with her.

When Jesus saw her, he really felt sorry for her, and said, "Dry your eyes." Then he walked up to the open coffin and said, "Young fellah—up!"

The dead man sat up, looked around, and started to talk. Jesus gave the young bloke back to his mum. Suddenly everyone just froze in their tracks... and then thanked God for what had happened.

They said, "You little beauty! Isn't God bonzer? And this Jesus bloke here is straight from God!" Soon everyone knew what had happened—even the dogs were barking it—all over the countryside.

John the Baptist again (Luke 7:18-35)

John the Baptist was told by his mates what the bush telegraph was saying about Jesus. So he sent a couple of them to ask Jesus, "Are you it? Are you the Promised One? Or should we stick around for someone else?"

So they rocked up to Jesus and said, "John the Baptist sent us, He said to ask: 'Are you it? Are you the Promised One? Or should we stick around for someone else?'"

At the time Jesus was busy healing—as busy as a one-armed paper-hanger in a gale—dealing with every kind of sickness in the medical dictionary.

Jesus replied, "Just tell John what you've seen: cripples up on their feet, blind blokes seeing, deaf blokes hearing, lepers clean (their sores gone), dead blokes out of the grave and walking around—and

God's message, God's good news, being announced. And, let me tell you this—well off is the bloke who's not crabby or spitting the dummy about me."

When those two had nicked off to deliver the reply, Jesus talked to the mob about John.

"What did you go out to the bush to see?" he said, "when you crowded around John? To see a blade of paspalum waving in the wind? No? Then what did you go to see? Someone dressed up like a pox doctor's clerk? Those sorts are in the towns, staying in the best pubs. So what did you go to see? A messenger from God? Too right! And more than just any messenger. John is the one God's Book talks about in these words: 'I'm sending my messenger ahead of you, to get things ready for you.' John is the first, number one, ahead of everyone who's ever lived. But... even the littlest kiddie in God's kingdom is ahead of John."

Now, just about everyone had listened to John. Even the corrupt tax collectors on the fiddle had done the right thing by changing their ways and asking John to baptise them. But the Pharisees and their self-righteous mates had turned their backs on God, and refused to be baptised by John.

Jesus went on, "What can I compare you lot with? You're little kids in a bad mood who can't be pleased. You're like kids sitting on the veranda shouting to each other: 'We played the fiddle and you wouldn't dance; we sang sad songs and you wouldn't cry.' John wouldn't go to your barbies or crack a tinnie with you, so you said: 'He's got a devil of a spirit in him—he's mad.' But I turn up at barbies and have a glass of chardonnay and you say I eat like a pig and drink like a fish, on top of which you say I've got really rough friends and hang out with the wrong crowd! Do you think that's wise? Do you think that's all that smart?"

Simon the Pharisee (Luke 7:36-50)

One of the Pharisees asked Jesus to pop in for a bite to eat. So he went and joined the others in the backyard, around the barbecue. A sheila with a reputation as the town bike heard he was there, and went to the house, taking a bottle of cologne with her.

Seeing Jesus she cried buckets. She washed his feet with her tears and dried them with her hair. Then she kissed his feet and put the cologne on them.

Now when the Pharisee, the host of the party, saw this he said to himself, "If this Jesus bloke really was a messenger from God he'd know what sort of sheila this is—he'd know her reputation is as rough as bags."

Jesus said to the Pharisee, "Simon, old son, I have something to say to you."

"Sure, what is it?" Simon replied.

"Picture this: two blokes owe some dough to a pawnbroker. One owes 500 quid and the other 50. Neither of them has a brass razoo—neither can pay. The pawnbroker says they don't have to—he just tears up their IOUs. Which of them will be really tickled?"

The Pharisee replied, "The one who owed the big bikkies."

"Too right," said Jesus. Then turning to the woman he said to Simon, "When I arrived you didn't give me the usual water and towel to wash my hands, but this woman has washed my feet with tears, and dried them with her hair, and kissed them, and even put expensive cologne on them. Her wrongdoings—of which there are heaps—are forgiven. You can understand why she's beside herself with gratitude. But the bloke who is not forgiven much, doesn't care much."

Then Jesus said to the woman, "Your wrongdoings are forgiven."

Simon's friends said to each other, "Who does this bloke think he is—forgiving people like this?"

Jesus said to the woman, "Because you trusted me, you are forgiven. I give you God's peace—peace of heart."

John the Baptist: his story ends *(Mark 6:17-29)*

King Herod had John the Baptist collared by the wallopers and chucked in the local lock-up because of his sister-in-law, Herodias (his brother Phil's better half). Herod was dead keen on this bird, and she shacked up with him.

John said, "What you've done is that wrong. It's not on."

This made Herodias as mad as a cut snake and she wanted John knocked off. But Herod was nervous because, although John was a wowser, he was a good bloke. And even though Herod was confused by what John said, he was glad to be earbashed by him.

Then Herod chucked a birthday wingding for himself, and invited all the toffs and big wigs.

When Herodias' daughter came in and bunged

on a show—danced for the party crowd—Herod was
dead pleased. He said to the young sheila, "Name
it and you can have it; up to half the acreage;
anything—just ask."

So this bird went out and asked her Mum,
"Whadda ya reckon I oughta ask for?" And with
an evil glint in her eye her Mum said, "The head of
John the Baptist."

So she toddled back into the party room and said,
"I want, right now, on a plate, the head of John the
Baptist."

This rattled old Herod, but he'd made the promise
in front of everyone and was stuck with it. He didn't
muck about, but straight away sent a big beefy
sergeant down to the lock-up to do the deed. Back
came John the Baptist's head—on a plate.

Herod gave it to the young sheila, who gave it to
her Mum.

When John's followers heard, they came and
collected the corpse and gave it a decent burial.

A gigantic picnic (Mark 6:31-44)

Jesus said to his team, "Come on out to the desert
for a bit, so you can have some kip." (There was
such a big mob hanging around they didn't even
have time for a bite to eat.)

They hopped in the skiff and rowed around the
shore to a quiet spot in the scrub. But the mob saw
them leave, and recognised them, and took off on
foot. So people from all the townships got there
ahead of them.

When Jesus came ashore he saw this enormous

mob, and felt sorry for them because they were like a bunch of aimless sheep with no one to keep an eye on them. He started talking to them, and gave them the good oil on a whole lot of things.

Late in the arvo his team came to him and said, "This is dry mallee country, and it's getting pretty late. Let the mob pop off so they can buy themselves some tucker from local properties or townships.

Jesus answered, "You feed them." They protested, "Do you want us to spend 200 smackers to buy enough bread for this lot?"

He said, "Well, how much bread is here? Go and check." They did so and said, "Five little pannikin loaves of damper—and a couple of fish."

Jesus ordered them all to sit down, in groups, on the cattle grass. The team ran around like kelpies and got them into groups of hundreds and fifties. Meanwhile, he took the damper and the fish, looked up to heaven, thanked God for the food, and broke the damper into bits, giving the bits to his team to share out. He did the same with the fish.

And everyone in the mob tucked into the bread and fish until they couldn't eat any more. Then they picked up the scraps—a dozen baskets full!

There were about 5,000 blokes in that mob.

Don't try this in your backyard pool! (Mark 6:45-52)

Jesus told his team to get into their boat straightaway and row across to Bethsaida (on the other side) while he sent the mob packing.

Having said toodle-oo to them, he went up into the hills to pray.

After dark the boat was in the middle of the lake, and Jesus was by himself on the shore. He could see they were in trouble, straining on the oars, struggling into the wind. In the early hours of the morning Jesus came across the lake. He was walking on the water, and about to pass the boat.

When the team saw him, walking on the water, they thought they'd seen a ghost. They yelped with surprise and were scared witless. Jesus said to them, "Calm down! And cheer up! It's me!" Then he climbed into the boat, and the wind died down.

They were knocked sideways. They were slow on the uptake, and didn't understand the meaning of what Jesus had done with the damper and the fish—or maybe they didn't want to understand.

Surgery is open *(Mark 6:53-56)*

They crossed over the lake to Gennesaret shire, and dropped anchor. When the team came ashore the locals recognised Jesus straight off and ran around like over-excited chooks.

The locals stretchered down all the sickies they could find to where they'd heard he was.

Whether in towns or cities or in the bush the locals would whip all the sickies into the main street where they begged Jesus just to let them touch the edge of his coat. And everyone that got touched, got better.

The old fogies *(Mark 7:1-13)*

A mob of Pharisees and lawyers from the Big Smoke (from Jerusalem) circled around Jesus having a go at him because, they said, his team didn't wash their hands before eating their tucker.

(The Pharisees lived the way their Jewish Mommas had taught them to live. They were dead kosher: washing their hands, having a bath after going to the markets, washing their cups and saucers and all the rest of the rules.)

These blokes asked Jesus: "Why's your team not strictly kosher like us? What's so hard about washing your hands already?"

Jesus replied, "Back in the old days Isaiah got it right when he said you're a bunch of shallow show-offs. In God's Book it says: 'their religion is all mouth and no trousers; their religion is a useless show; they flog their own ideas like it's God's truth.' You turn your backs on God and push your own rules.

"Didn't Moses tell you to respect your Mum and Dad? And didn't he say that anyone who didn't was as good as dead? But you twist this by saying that if a bloke's got something that would help his Mum and Dad he can say it's been 'promised to God'—and then he doesn't have to help them. In heaps of ways, just like that, you've twisted God's message with your own little rules."

Unclean! Unclean! (Mark 7:14-23)

Jesus called the mob together and said, "Open your ears and pay attention. It's not what goes into your mouth that makes you unclean in God's eyes, but what comes out. Get it?"

After Jesus had slipped into a bungalow away

from the mob his team said they didn't get it, and what did he mean? Jesus said: "Still a bit slow on the uptake, eh? Look, the tucker you eat can't make you unclean—it goes into your tummy (not your heart) then through the guts and down the sewer." By this Jesus meant that all types of tucker was okay to eat.

Then Jesus said:

"It's what comes out of the 'inner you' that makes you unclean. It's inside yourself that you cook up evil thoughts, vulgar deeds, stealing, murder, adultery, greed, meanness, deceit, perving, envy, rudeness, pride, and sheer stupidity. It's this stuff inside your head that looks to God like disgusting filth."

Everybody needs good neighbours (Luke 10:25-37)

One of the lawyers chipped in to test Jesus with a question. "Teacher," this smart alec said, "What've I gotta do to score eternal life?"

Jesus replied, "What's in God's Book? How do you read it?"

The lawyer shrugged his shoulders and said, "Well, you know, the Bible says: 'Love the Lord your God with all your heart, soul, strength, and mind.' It also says, 'Love your neighbour as much as you love yourself.'"

"Spot on," Jesus responded. "Do that and you'll score eternal life."

Sticking out his chest, and with a smart gleam in his eye, the lawyer said, "All right then, just who is my neighbour? Answer me that!"

Jesus replied by telling this story:

"A certain bloke was taking the Jerusalem Road to Jericho. A bunch of bushrangers attacked him, stole his dough, and left him as good as dead. A big-wig from the Temple happened to pass by, took one look at the bloke, crossed the road and hurried off. Another official who was on the road that day did the same.

"Then a really ordinary bloke (a grubby old street sweeper you wouldn't look twice at) passed by and felt really sorry for him. So he used his first aid kit to patch him up, and then put him on his old nag, took him to the nearest pub, and took care of him. The next day he gave the barman some dough and said, 'Look after this bloke. And if he costs more than this I'll pay the rest on my way back.'"

Then Jesus asked: "Who was the neighbour in that story?"

The lawyer said, "Well, the bloke who looked after the victim, I guess."

"Too right," said Jesus, "Now you go and live like that!"

Who is this bloke? (Mark 8:27-30)

Jesus and the team were visiting the townships around Caesarea Philippi. As they made their way down the track one day Jesus said to the team, "Who do the mob say I am?"

The team told him, "Some blokes say you're John the Baptist, or maybe that old timer Elijah back again. Other blokes reckon you're one of the prophets."

Then Jesus stopped and said, "But who do you say I am?"

Peter replied, "You are... the Christ! The Promised One!"

Jesus then warned them not to spill the beans to anyone about this, just yet.

And what's he come to do? (Mark 8:31-9:1)

Jesus began telling them what was in store for him: basically a lot of suffering (rejected by the crew in power), a gruesome death, and then coming back to life again. Jesus spelled it all out.

Peter took Jesus to one side and told him to stop saying such horrible things. But when he turned around and saw the team all listening he chipped Peter: "That's a devilish thing to say! Look at it from God's point of view, not the spin doctors."

Then he called everyone who was travelling with him and the team and said:

"If you want to follow me, forget about yourself. Take up your cross and follow in my footsteps. If you want to save your life, then give it away. Whoever gives up his life for me, and for the news about me, will end up with more life than he can imagine. What would be the point of getting the world, but losing yourself in the process? What price would you pay for your own soul?

"Don't turn your back on me and my message because of the know-it-alls and cynics around you. If you do, I'll turn my back on you when the day comes for me to stand in God's glory and power.

"The truth is that there are some people here today who will see that glory and power before they die."

Cosmic power on display *(Mark 9:2-13)*

Six days later Jesus took Peter, Jim and John with him up to the high country—where they *did* see his cosmic glory and power. Jesus changed in front of their eyes. It was like something out of a movie: as though he was filled with light, dazzling like the sun itself.

Then two heroes from the old days, Moses and Elijah, came into view beside Jesus, talking to him.

Peter blurted out, "Master, it's terrific to be here! Let's... ah... mark these three spots... ah... for you and Moses and Elijah." Peter didn't have a clue what to say, because, like the others, he was terrified.

Suddenly there was a huge, billowing cloud overhead, and from deep inside the cloud came a Voice saying: "This is my Beloved Son! When he speaks, listen!"

Then, just as suddenly, they were alone again, and the three of them could see only Jesus and the mountainside.

On the way down Jesus told them not to breath a word about this until after he'd come back to life. So they kept it to themselves, but they argued with each other about what he might mean by "come back to life".

They asked Jesus, "Why do the Bible teachers say that Elijah has to turn up first—before the Christ, the Promised One?"

Jesus said, "They're right that Elijah comes first. But what does the Bible say about the Promised One? That he'll suffer badly, and be treated with contempt. Well, Elijah *did* come—and they gave *him* the rough end of the stick too."

A sick boy *(Mark 9:14-29)*

When they got back down to where the rest of the team was they saw a mob surrounding them, and some religious big wigs arguing with them.

The mob was surprised to see Jesus and ran up to say "G'day." He asked, "What's this all about?"

One of the blokes said, "Master, I brought my son to see you. He's been invaded by a spirit that stops him speaking, and when he gets an attack he has a fit, and foams at the mouth and grinds his teeth, and then becomes rigid. I asked your team to get rid of the invading spirit and they were dead useless."

Jesus said, "What's wrong with you people? You've got no trust at all, have you? You're a real trial, you are. Bring the kid here."

They brought the kid over, but as soon as the spirit saw Jesus he threw the kid into convulsions, thrashing about like mad.

Jesus asked the boy's Dad, "How long has he been like this?"

"Ever since he was a toddler," the man replied. "It's really destructive—it's thrown him into fires and into the water quite often. Please, *please* help us... if you can."

Jesus replied, "What's this 'if' business? Anything

is possible when you trust me."

The boy's Dad said, "I *do* trust you—a bit. Help me trust you a lot—completely and totally."

When Jesus saw more and more people crowding around he gave the invading spirit a blast: "Out! That's an order! And never come back!"

The spirit made the kid scream and tremble—and then left. The boy fainted, and everyone said he'd carked it. But Jesus took his hand and helped him up.

When Jesus and the team were alone they asked, "Why couldn't we do that?"

"It needs prayer," Jesus replied, "a total dependence on God."

Death again *(Mark 9:30-32)*

Jesus and his team set off through Galilee shire, not telling anyone where they were going, because he was teaching his team.

He said, "I'm going to be betrayed to some people—enemies of God. I'll be murdered, and three days later come back to life."

The team didn't know what he meant, but they were afraid to ask.

The tale of the lost sheep *(Luke 15:1-7)*

Con men, illywhackers and low-lifes hung around listening to Jesus. So the Pharisees and the lawyers started whinging, "This bloke mixes with the scum. He'll even have a pizza with them!" So Jesus told them this story:

"What sort of bloke who has a flock of 100 sheep

and lost one of them, wouldn't leave the other 99
in the home yard and search the paddocks until he
found the missing merino? And when he gets back
home he'll say: 'Hey, let's crack a tinnie! I found that
merino of mine that went missing!'"

Jesus said: "Just like that, there's more barracking
and cheering in heaven over one wrongdoer who
turns back to God, than over 99 who think they
don't have to!"

The tale of the lost coin (Luke 15:8-10)

Jesus told the people another story:

"What will an old lady do if her life savings
consists of ten coins, and she loses one of them?
She'll turn on all the lights, and sweep out the place
like she's never done before, and look in every
corner till she finds it. Then she'll call up all the
other old ladies and say, "Guess what! I found that
coin I thought I'd lost!"

Jesus said, "Just like that, God's angels are tickled
pink when even one person turns back to him."

The tale of the lost son (Luke 15:11-32)

Then Jesus told the people another story:

This bloke had two sons. The youngest said,
"Dad, how about letting me have my half of what
I'll get in your will—right now."

So the old man shared out his property between
the two boys. The youngest immediately sold his
half, and took off for distant parts, where he had
a wild time, while the money just ran through his

fingers. When he was broke a drought hit that spot, and pretty soon he was on the breadline.

He got a job feeding slops to pigs, and was so hungry he would have been happy to eat the slops himself!

He finally came to his senses, and said, "My Dad's farm hands live better than this! I'll go back home, and I'll say: 'Dad, I've done the wrong thing by you (and by God). I'm not good enough to be a son of yours anymore, but I'll come back and work for you as a farm hand... if you'll have me.'"

So he set off.

His home farm was still a long way down the road when his Dad spotted him, ran to him, and hugged him and shook his hand. The boy said: 'Dad, I've done the wrong thing by you (and by God). I'm not good enough to be a son of yours anymore..."

But his Dad called out, "Hey! Get out some clean clothes for this boy. And some decent shoes. Heat up the barbie and crack a keg! My boy was as good as dead, but now he's back! He was lost, but here he is!"

And so they began to party.

The boy's big brother was out in the top paddock, and as he rode back home he could hear the noise of the party. So he called over one of the blokes and said, "What's going on here?" This bloke explained, "Your little brother's back home, safe and sound, so your Dad's turned on a party with the spit-roast going and a keg and everything." Big brother blew a fuse, and refused to even go into the house.

His Dad came out and said, "Please—come on in." But big brother whinged, "For years I've slaved out here and done what you wanted. You never put on a barbie for me and my friends—not even a few lamb chops! Now this boy of yours drags himself back home, having chucked away all his dough on whores, and you do this! The big party! The spit-roast! The keg!"

His Dad said, "Oh, my son, I do appreciate you. And look around you—all of this is yours. But we've got to have a party today! Your brother was as good as dead, but now he's back! He was lost, but here he is!"

Jesus hits the big smoke *(Mark 11:1-11)*

As Jesus and his team reached the outskirts of Jerusalem (around Bethphage and Bethany, at Mount Olive) he sent two of them on ahead.

"Pop down to the next town," he told them. "As soon as you arrive you'll see a nag—a young horse that's never been ridden. Untie it and bring it here. If anyone asks you what's going on, just say, 'The Master needs it—it'll be back soon.'"

They nicked off to the next town and found the nag by a doorway, in the main street. Some blokes who were hanging around said, "Whaddya think ya doin' with that nag?"

They repeated what Jesus had said, and the blokes said, "Orright then."

They brought the nag back to Jesus, threw some coats on its back, and Jesus sat on the beast. Some of the mob got excited and threw branches from palm trees, and even their own coats, on the ground.

As Jesus rode into Jerusalem the mob was barracking and cheering:

"Onya Jesus!"

"Onya God!

"Go Jesus!"

"He's God's Promised One!"

"The new King David!"

"Onya God! Whadda bewdy!"

When Jesus arrived in Jerusalem he went straight to the Temple and took a squiz at everything, but because it was already late in the arvo he went back to Bethany with the team.

The fig tree (Mark 11:12-14)

Next morning on the way to Jerusalem Jesus was feeling peckish. He saw a fig tree with nothing but leaves (it wasn't fig season yet). Jesus said to the tree: "You've grown your last fig". The team heard him say it.

In the temple (Mark 11:15-19)

In Jerusalem Jesus went straight to the Temple. There he did his lolly at all the market stalls. He tipped over their stalls and chased out the dealers. He stopped the carriers carting their goods through the Temple. He shouted, "The Bible says: 'My house shall be called a house of prayer for all nations'—but you've turned it into a thieves' kitchen!"

The head honchos and their lawyers heard all this and started plotting to have him knocked off. But they were afraid of his popularity, because he was such a respected teacher.

That evening Jesus and the team left the city again.

The fig tree again (Mark 20:-26)

Next morning they walked passed the same fig tree and noticed that it was shrivelled up, roots and all. Peter remembered what Jesus had said to it the day before. He said, "Master, look what's happened to the tree you put the curse on."

Jesus said to his team:

"Trust God. If you tell a mountain to shift itself into the sea, and trust God (without a shadow of a doubt)—it'll happen. So what I'm saying is: when you say your prayers, trust God—and he'll give you his very best.

"And when you do say your prayers you've got to forgive everyone who's offended you, so that God (your loving heavenly Father) will forgive you for all the ways you've offended him."

The lawyers grill Jesus (Mark 11:27-33)

Jesus and his team returned to Jerusalem, and to the Temple. The head honchos and their lawyers came over to him and asked, "What right have you got to carry on like this? Who gave you this authority?"

Jesus replied, "First I have a question for you. You answer my question, then I'll answer yours. Who gave John the Baptist the right to baptise? Was it God? Or was it just his own idea?"

This put the cat among the pigeons, and they said to each other, "We can't say it was God, or Jesus will ask why we didn't believe him, and let him baptise us. On the other hand, this mob thinks John was a real prophet, so we can't say it was all his own idea."

They were scared of the mob, so they told Jesus, "We have no idea, actually."

Jesus responded, "Well, in that case I won't tell you where my authority comes from."

The nasty tenants (Mark 12:1-12)

Then Jesus told them this story:

A certain squatter had a big property. He put in stockyards, fences, artesian bores and all the rest. Then he rented the place out to a bunch of tenant farmers, and left.

At harvest time he sent his overseer to collect the rent. The tenants grabbed the overseer, gave him a good thrashing and sent him away empty handed.

The squatter then sent one of his drovers, but they bashed this bloke up too, and gave him a proper tongue lashing. Then the squatter sent another—and this one they actually killed. He kept sending one stockman after another. Some they bashed, some they killed.

Finally the squatter sent his son, who he loved very much. He thought they'd respect his son. But the tenants said to themselves: "Someday he'll own this property. Let's kill him, then the whole farm can be ours!" So they grabbed the squatter's son and killed him, and threw his body out on the road.

After telling this story, Jesus said: "What do you imagine that squatter will do? He'll come with the troopers, arrest those tenants, and someone else will get the property. The Bible says: 'The brick the builders chucked aside has become the most important brick in the building. This is something God has done, and it's staggering.'"

The head honchos knew it was them he was talking about, and would have arrested him on the spot except that they were afraid of the mob, so they let him alone, and nicked off.

Another trick question (Mark 12:13-17)

The Pharisees put their heads together with some of King Herod's cronies. They sent some blokes to trick Jesus into putting his foot in it. They went to him and said, "Teacher, you're an honest man. You don't shape what you say to suit popular opinion, but you tell the truth of God: so then, should we pay taxes to the Emperor or not?"

But Jesus was on to them, and said, "Trying to catch me out, are you? Show me a coin."

They brought him a coin, and he said, "Whose head is stamped on this coin?"

"The Emperor's," they said, "Caesar's."

"Spot on," said Jesus. "So give Caesar what's his, and give God what's his."

They found this pretty breath taking.

Life after death (Mark 12:18-27)

The Sadducees are a bunch who don't believe in life after death. So some of them tried to bowl a bouncer at Jesus, and said:

"Teacher, Moses wrote that if a married man dies and leaves no kiddies, his brother should marry the widow. The idea being that their first son would then be thought of as the son of the dead brother. Well, there were once seven brothers, see. The first one married, but died without kids. The second brother married his brother's widow, and he also tumbled off the twig without having kids. The same thing happened to the third brother, and finally to all seven brothers. (Not a lucky family, when ya think about it!) At last the woman died. When God raises people back to life, whose wife will this sheila be? After all, she had been married to all seven of those brothers."

Jesus replied:

"You're as thick as three short planks! And you don't know your Bible! And you don't understand the power of God! When God raises people to life they're not married and they don't marry. They're like the angels in heaven. But about this business of life after death: don't you remember from the Bible, when God spoke to Moses out of the burning bush he said, 'I am the God of Abraham, Isaac and Jacob'? He's the God of the living, not the dead—so you're dead wrong!'

The main rules *(Mark 12:28-34)*

A lawyer rolled up while Jesus and the Sadducees were having this argy-bargy. When he heard Jesus giving such neat answers he asked, "What's the most important rule for living?"

Jesus replied, "Top of the list is this: 'You have only one Lord and God. You must love him with all your heart, soul, mind, and strength.' The second most important one says: 'Love others as much as you love yourself.' Nothing else measures up to these two."

The man responded, "Teacher, you're spot on when you say there's only one God, and we oughta love him with the whole of our hearts, and brains, and energy, and that we oughta love our neighbours like we love ourselves. These things matter more than being 'done' by the priest in some ritual in church."

When Jesus heard these sensible words he said, 'You're not a million miles away from God's Kingdom!'

After this no one was game to ask him any questions.

The "official" teachers (Mark 12:35-40)

When Jesus was giving a talk in the plaza of the Temple he said, "How can the officials make out that the Christ (the Promised One) is King David's great-great-great-(etcetera)-grandson? Old David himself (given the words by God's Spirit) wrote: 'The Lord God said to *my* Lord: come and stand by me while I make your enemies grovel at your feet.' If King David called the Christ *his* Lord how can he be David's great-great-great-(etcetera)-grandson?"

The mob loved hearing Jesus talk.

In one of his talks he said: "Keep a wary eye on the 'official' teachers. They like to swan about in flash clothes, and sit in the box seats at the Meeting Halls, and have a spot on the top table at the best dinner parties. But they'll foreclose on a widow's mortgage, and then go and pray a long, loud prayer. They'll really cop it from God!"

Who gives most? *(Mark 12:41-44)*

Jesus was sitting near the Temple offering box. He saw the rich sticking in wads of folding money, and then a widow, an old duck on the pension, drop in a couple of coins—just small change.

Jesus called his team to gather round and said: "Straight up, this old lady put in more than all the rest, because the rest who kicked the kitty just stuck in what they could spare, while she put in her grocery money.'

Things to come *(Mark 13:1-23)*

As they were leaving the Temple one of the team said to him, "Don't you just love this building? The design! The huge stones!"

Jesus replied: "Take a good look. It won't last. This place will end up a heap of rubble."

Later Peter, John, Jim and Andy came to Jesus on Mount Olive (on the slope facing the Temple) and asked, "When will this destruction happen? Will there be any warning signs?"

Jesus replied: "Keep your eyes open! Don't let anyone fool you! Lots of blokes will bung on an act, and say: 'Jesus sent me.' People will be fooled.

"When the news is full of wars and war mongering, don't lose your head. These things happen, but it's not the end of the world. One lot will attack another, and then be attacked themselves. There'll be earthquakes, famines... all that stuff. But that's just the beginning, not the end.

"But watch it! You'll be arrested and dragged into court, or given a really rough time in the Meeting Halls. Sometimes you'll be dragged before tin-pot presidents and power mad magistrates. Stand up for me, and my message. Before the end comes, the message about me has to be told around the world.

"When you're dragged before some tribunal, don't panic! Don't get nervous about what to say, because God can speak through you—he can put words in your mouth.

"Your own relatives will betray you, and families will be divided. Everyone will look on you as some sort of mug, because of me and my message. But if you stick with me to the bitter end you'll be okay—and okay forever!

"When a real monster turns up, don't hang around! (Work out what this means for yourself.) People in Judea when the monster arrives should clear off to the hills. If you're working on the roof don't go back into the house—just go! If you're out in the paddock, don't go back for your stuff—just go! For expectant Mums and nursing Mums it'll be terrible. Just pray it doesn't happen in the dead of winter. What's coming at that time, in this place, will be the worst time in the world—ever. Unless God cuts it short no one will survive. But for the sake of his faithful few, God *will* cut it short.

"If some clown says, "Here's the Promised One!' or 'There he is!'—use your loaf, and don't believe him. Because pretenders and liars will turn up, doing signs and wonders, and trying to lead even God's faithful few down a blind alley. So, be on your guard. Don't say I haven't warned you."

Before "The End" is written (Mark 13:24-37)

Jesus told them:

> Before the suffering will end,
> The sun itself will descend.
> Alarm bells will chime,
> Yet the moon will not shine.
> The whole cosmos will cry,
> And stars fall from the sky.

"Then," said Jesus, "then I'll be seen, surrounded by clouds of power and glory. I shall send out my Messengers to gather my people from the four corners of the world—from all over the shop.

"There's a lesson to be learned from the humble fig tree: its new leaves tell you summer's coming. When you see all this happening, you'll know the clock is ticking, and the countdown has begun. And you will see it happen! Remember: even planets and suns finally die—but my words live forever.

"And no one knows when 'The End' gets written in the big book! Not the angels! Not even me! God alone knows, and that's a fact. So, stay on your toes, and keep your eyes open. It's like when the boss goes away on a trip and leaves the staff in charge—each with their own job to do. Stick to your duty, and keep your eyes peeled because you don't know when The Boss is coming back! It might be tomorrow, or the day after, or next week, or... whenever. So don't slack off.

"Pass this message on to everyone else, and stay alert!"

The death plot begins *(Mark 14:1-11)*

It was now two days before the big do called the Passover, and the head honchos and lawyers put their heads together to cook up a way to lay their hands on Jesus, and have him killed. They said, "We've got to watch out what we do during the big festival, because the mob might go bananas."

Meanwhile, Jesus was having dinner at Simon's home in Bethany. (Simon's the one who used to have leprosy.) During dinner a sheila came up with a bottle of this really expensive perfume. She opened it up and splashed the contents of the bottle on Jesus.

All around the table people complained, "What a waste! That could have been sold for a stack of dough, and given to the poor."

But Jesus said, "Let her alone. This is a good thing she's done. You can look after the poor any time. But I won't always be here. She's done what she could. She's prepared my body, ahead of time, for its burial. And, honestly, wherever the message about me is heard around the world, what's she's done today will be heard about too."

Judas Iscariot, who was one of the team, went slinking off to the head honchos, to turn Jesus in. They were delighted and offered him a blank cheque, so he promised to keep his eyes open for the right moment.

A last meal together (Mark 14:12-26)

It was the first day of the Festival when they traditionally ate the Lebanese bread and roast lamb. The team said to Jesus, "Where are we having dinner?"

Jesus said to two of the team, "Pop into the city and you'll see a bloke carrying a drum of water. Follow him. See which house he goes into, and say to the owner, 'The Master sent us to check out the guest room for tonight's dinner.' He'll take you upstairs and show you a large dining room. You can get the dinner ready there."

The two went into town, and it all happened just the way Jesus said. So they prepared the dinner.

That night Jesus and the rest of the team joined them. While they were eating Jesus said, "One of the blokes at this table is planning to betray me."

This plunged the team into gloom, and they said things like: "Surely not!" and "Not me, at least!"

Jesus said: "It's one of the team—one who's eating with me right now. I will die, just as the Bible predicted. But it will be hard yards for my betrayer. It would be better for that bloke if he'd never been born."

While they were eating Jesus took some of the bread, broke it, gave thanks to God for it, and said, "My body is just like this bread," and he gave it to them.

Then he poured out a glass of wine, gave thanks to God for it, and as he handed the wine around he said, "This wine is like my blood, which is poured out for many people—the blood that seals my last will and testament. This is the last glass of wine I'll have until I drink the new wine in God's Kingdom."

Then they sang a song together, and went out to Mount Olive.

Peter's boast (Mark 14:27-31)

Jesus said to the team: "You'll all fail me. The Bible predicts: 'I will strike the shepherd, and the sheep will scatter.' But after I come back to life again, I'll meet you in Galilee."

Peter protested, "The rest of them might fail you, but not me."

Jesus said to him, "Honestly, before sunrise—before the rooster crows twice—three times you'll deny even knowing me."

Peter spluttered, "But... but... I'll die before I do that!"

And the others all said the same thing.

Jesus prays (Mark 14:31-42)

Jesus and his team came to a spot among the olive trees called Gethsemane. He said to them, "Wait here for me, while I go and pray."

He took Peter, John and Jim with him. His heart was in his boots. "I feel like death," he said. "Stay here, and keep me company."

He went on a little further alone, and then sank

to the ground, and began to pray that if it were at all possible, what he was facing would not happen.

"Father, Father," he groaned, "you can do anything. Can I avoid this horror that's coming? But, in the end, it's got to be what you want, not what I want."

Finally he returned to the other three, and found them sleeping.

"Peter!" he said, "Asleep? Was an hour too long to ask you to wait? Stay on guard and pray or you'll be overwhelmed. I'm sure the spirit is willing enough, but mere flesh and blood is weak."

He went off again, and prayed the same prayer, using the same words.

When he returned he again found them sound asleep. This time they were embarrassed and didn't know what to say.

Then a third time it happened, and when he returned Jesus said, "Still sleeping? Enough! This is it. The time has come for me to be handed over to the evil schemers. Let's go, the traitor's almost here."

The arrest (Mark 14:43-50)

As he said these words Judas the traitor (one of the team) arrived leading a mob of blokes armed to the teeth with swords and clubs. They'd been sent by the head honchos and the lawyers. Judas the traitor had tipped them off: "Arrest the bloke I walk straight up to and kiss on the cheek. He's the one. Grab him and put him under guard."

So Judas walked straight up to Jesus, and said,

"Master!" and kissed him on the cheek.

The guards rushed forward and grabbed Jesus by the arms. One of Jesus' team swung a sword wildly and lopped off the ear of one of the guards (one who was on the staff of the High Priest).

Jesus said, "Am I some sort of thug or blagger that you have to come out armed to the teeth to arrest me? I've been down in the Temple, giving talks, every day—you could have arrested me there. But it's happened this way to fulfil the predictions in the Bible."

At that point all the remaining members of Jesus' team turned tail and ran. One was a young bloke who was wearing only a toga. When the guards grabbed at his toga he left it behind and ran off naked.

The trial—part one (Mark 14:53-65)

They took Jesus off to the High Priest's palace where the head honchos, the community leaders, and the lawyers were gathered waiting for him.

Peter followed—at a distance. In the palace courtyard the guards had built a small campfire, and Peter sat down with them there, to keep warm.

Inside, the whole council was trying to find some scrap of evidence against Jesus so they could ask for the death penalty, but they were having trouble. The professional perjurers they lined up kept contradicting each other. Finally, some blokes who couldn't lie straight in bed got up and said: "We heard this character say he'd pull down our Temple. And he said that in three days he'd magically build another one." But they still couldn't get their stories straight!

Then the High Priest got up and said to Jesus, "Well? What about it? Have you got anything to say for yourself?"

Jesus said nothing.

So the High Priest said, "Well, then, are you, or are you not, the Christ, the Promised One? Are you, or are you not, God's own Son?"

Jesus said: "I am. And you shall see me in my glory and power, lifted up in the clouds."

At this the High Priest spat the dummy, and did his lolly completely: "Did you hear that? Did you hear that? Who needs witnesses? You heard what he said! He insulted God! Come on, what do you say about that?"

And they all voted for the death penalty.

Then these "community leaders" gathered around Jesus and began to spit on him, and punch him. They blindfolded him, and slapped him, and said: "Prophesy then—go on! Who hit you?"

They were still hitting him as they led him away.

Peter's cowardice (Mark 14:66-72)

Meanwhile, Peter was around the fire in the courtyard below. A girl who worked in the kitchens saw him and said, "I know you! I've seen you hanging around with that Jesus from Nazareth."

Peter denied it. "I don't know what you're talking about!" he protested. "And you don't know what you're talking about either!"

He moved a bit further away, but the girl said to some of the guards, "This bloke's one of them." Peter shook his head, and said, "No, no—not a chance."

But then one of the guards said, "You've got that funny accent—you are from Galilee." Peter began to curse and swear (just like a fisherman!) and half shouted: "I don't even know this bloke you're talking about!"

At that moment a rooster crowed—for the second time. Then Peter remembered those words of Jesus, "before sunrise—before the rooster crows twice—three times you'll deny even knowing me."

Peter rushed out into the darkness, and broke down in tears.

The trial—part two (Mark 15:1-15)

At the crack of dawn the head honchos, the community leaders and the lawyers held a formal meeting as a council. They had Jesus tied up and marched him off to Governor Pilate.

The Governor said to Jesus: "Well then, are you the King of the Jews?"

Jesus replied: "You said it."

Pilate said, "Just give me a straight answer! Look at the charge sheet they've brought against you."

But Jesus said nothing further, and Pilate was puzzled.

During the Festival Pilate always released one prisoner—just to please the mob. At the time his army had a bloke named Barabbas locked up. He'd been arrested as a terrorist and charged with murder.

The crowd started yelling that it was Festival time, time for Pilate to set a prisoner free.

So Pilate asked them, "What about this bloke here? Do you want me to set free the King of the Jews?"

But the head honchos had their rent-a-crowd mingled through the mob, and they all yelled out for Barabbas to be released.

"Alright then," said Pilate, "but what about this other one—the one you tell me is the King of the Jews?"

"Kill him!" the mob screamed. "Kill him!"

"But what's he done?" shouted Pilate. "I can't figure it out. What on earth has he done?"

But the mob set up a chant of: "Kill him! Kill him!"

Governor Pilate wanted to please the crowd, so he released Barabbas, had Jesus whipped, and then passed the death sentence on him.

The execution (Mark 15:16-32)

The Roman soldiers led Jesus inside the courtyard of the Governor's palace, where they called out the whole regiment.

The dressed him up in fancy dress—something like a king's robe—and put a pretend crown made of thorn branches on his head. Then they danced around, mocked him and made fun of him. "Oh, King of the Jews! Oh, dear King!" they hooted. They hit him, spat on him, and then knelt down and pretended to worship him.

When they'd had their fun, they took the fancy dress off him, put him in his own clothes again, and the execution squad marched him out. On the way they grabbed a bloke out of the crowd (a visitor from Cyrene named Simon, the Dad of Alex and Rufus) and made him carry the wooden cross.

They brought Jesus to Skull Rock, the execution site. They offered him drugged wine, but he knocked it back.

Then they nailed him to the wooden cross.

The execution squad played dice to see who'd get which bit of his clothing. It was nine o'clock in the morning.

They tacked a sign to his cross showing the charge against him. It said: "The King of the Jews."

Jesus was executed between two thieves—one on either side. And the crowd made fun of Jesus, jeering: "Hey you—who can knock down Temples and re-build them in three days—show us how smart you are: get off your cross! Come on down!"

The head honchos and the lawyers were there, having their bit of fun, saying to each other, "He rescued others, let's see him rescue himself. Let's see this 'King of the Jews' get off his cross. Of course, if you do that, O Promised One, then we'll believe you!" And the dying thieves joined in the mockery.

The death *(Mark 15:33-41)*

At midday the sky turned dark, and the shadow remained until three o'clock in the afternoon.

At about that time Jesus cried out (in Aramaic): "Eloi, Eloi, lama sabachthani." (Which means: "My God! My God! Why have you left me?")

Someone in the mob said, "Listen—he's calling out to Elijah." Another man got some wine in a sponge and held it up for him to drink, saying, "Let's see if Elijah comes and takes him down."

Then Jesus gave a loud cry, and breathed his last.

At that moment the great curtain of the Inner Temple tore in two—from top to bottom.

The sergeant, in charge of the execution squad, standing right in front of Jesus, saw him die and said, "It's true! This man was God's own Son!"

At the back of the crowd were some Galilean women who had come to Jerusalem with Jesus: Mary Magdalene, Mary (Jim and John's Mum), Salome, and others.

The burial (Mark 15:42-47)

It was nearly sunset, and everything was about to shut down for the official day off. A bloke from Arimathea, named Joseph (a member of the city council, and a devout bloke who looked forward to God's Kingdom) had the gumption to go to Governor Pilate and ask to be given the body of Jesus.

The Governor was a bit startled to hear that Jesus was already dead, so he called in the sergeant from the execution squad to check.

When the sergeant reported that he'd double-checked and Jesus was really dead—dead as a doornail—Pilate said Joseph could have the body.

Joseph brought a long burial sheet, took the body down from the cross, wrapped the body in the sheet, and buried it in a nearby tomb newly cut in the rock. He rolled a heavy stone in place to seal the tomb.

The two Marys who'd seen Jesus die were there, and saw the burial.

Jesus is alive! (John 20:1-10)

On Sunday morning, before sunrise, Mary Magdalene set off for the tomb. She found the heavy stone that had sealed the entrance rolled away.

At this she took off like a rabbit and ran back to where the team was staying. She found Peter, and that other team member who was a good mate of Jesus, and puffed out, "He's gone! Someone's taken him! And I don't know where!"

Peter and the other bloke took off for the tomb at top speed. The other bloke got there first and looked inside. Sure enough, apart from the burial sheet the tomb was empty. Then Peter caught up, went inside, and saw the empty tomb, and the burial sheet, with the cloth that had been wound around the head of the corpse lying separately.

The other bloke came in after Peter, saw all of this, and he was the first one to believe what had happened—even though, at the time they didn't understand that the Bible said that Jesus would come back from the dead.

Mary sees Jesus (John 20:11-18)

Mary was standing in the garden, outside the tomb, crying her eyes out. Still crying, she stooped down and looked inside. She saw two angels in white, one sitting where the head would have been and the other where the feet would have been.

"Now then," they said, "why all these tears?"

"They've taken him," she sobbed. "The Master's been taken. And I don't know where."

As she said this she turned back to the garden and saw Jesus standing there, without knowing it was Jesus.

"Now then," he said to her, "why all these tears? Who are you looking for?"

Taking him for the gardener she sobbed, "Oh, please, if you took him, just tell me where—and I'll come and fetch him."

Jesus said to her, "Mary!"

She turned to face him and cried out, "Teacher!"

He said, "Now, now, don't cling to me like that. I've got to go. I've got to go to the Father. But you whiz back to the team and tell them that I'm going to My Father and your Father, to My God and your God."

Mary rushed back and told the others that she'd seen the Master. And she told them what he'd said.

Others see Jesus *(John 20:19-23)*

That same day (a Sunday) at sunset, when the team was in hiding in the house with all the doors shut (because they were still afraid of the Temple authorities) Jesus came.

He stood in the middle of the room, greeted them with the word, "Peace!" and then showed them the wounds in his hands and in his side.

They were beside themselves with excitement and happiness to see the Master.

Again Jesus said, "Peace be with you!" adding, "Just as the Father sent me, so I'm sending you." Taking a deep breath he said, "Receive my Spirit. If you forgive someone's wrongdoings they're forgiven. If you don't, they aren't."

Thomas sees Jesus (John 20:24-29)

Although Thomas (who was a twin) was one of the team he wasn't with them that night. So when the others said, "Hey! We've see the Lord!" Tom said, "Pull the other leg! Unless I see the nail wounds in his hands—and *touch them*—and the wound in his side too—I just won't believe it!"

Eight days later they were together again, and Tom was with them this time. And Jesus came, even though the doors were shut, and stood in the middle of the room and greeted them.

Then Jesus said to Thomas, "Come on—reach out your hand and touch these wounds—in my hands and my side. Give up your niggling doubts, and trust me!"

Thomas was gob smacked and said, "You are my Lord—and my God!"

Jesus said, "You trust me because you've seen me. But really well off are those who haven't seen me, but trust me just the same."

The purpose (John 20:30-31)

All of this has been written down so that you can trust Jesus as the Promised One, the Christ, God's own Son. And so that—by trusting him, personally—

you can have real life (with God, starting here and now, and going on... forever!).

His mates see Jesus *(John 21:1-14)*

A bit later Jesus' mates saw him on the shore of Lake Tiberias. It was like this.

There was a bunch of them there: Peter, Tom, Nathan, the two Zebedee boys, and a couple of others.

Peter said, "I'm going to do a spot of fishing."

"Good idea," said the others, "we'll come too."

So they went out in the boat, fished all night, and didn't even catch a tiddler.

About sunrise the next morning Jesus stood on the shore (but they didn't recognise him). He called out, "Caught anything?"

"Nope, not a thing" they shouted.

So he called out, "Drop your net over the right side of the boat—try again."

They did what he said, and this time the net was so full they couldn't pull the thing back into the boat. John said to Peter, "Hey! It's the Lord!"

When Peter heard it was the Lord he grabbed the coat he'd taken off (when he was working), jumped into the water, and headed for shore. The others stayed in the boat (about 100 metres out) and, dragging the full net behind them, rowed back in.

When they landed they found a campfire going and fish and bread already cooking. Jesus said, "Fetch some of the fish you've just caught."

It was Peter who dragged the net up on to the

beach. They counted the fish: 153 whoppers! And the net didn't rip!

"Come on," said Jesus, "breakfast's on." None of them was game enough to say, "Who are you?" knowing it was Him.

Jesus shared out the fresh bread and the barbecued fish. This was the third time they'd seen him since he'd come back from the dead.

Jesus and Peter (John 21:15-19)

After breakfast Jesus turned to Peter and asked, "Peter Johnson—do you love me more than these others do?"

Peter said, "You bet! Too right!"

"Then feed my lambs."

A second time Jesus said, "Peter Johnson—do you love me more than these others do?"

Peter said, "Yes, Master—you know I do."

"Then look after my sheep."

A third time Jesus said, "Peter Johnson—do you love me more than these others do?"

Peter was really cut because he'd been asked this question three times. He replied, "Master, you know everything—so you know I love you."

"Then feed my sheep," Jesus said. Then he added, "when you were young you dressed yourself and went wherever you wanted. When you're old you'll hold out your arms, others will dress you, and they'll take you where you don't want to go." Jesus said this to let Peter know what kind of death he would die, and that his death would point people to God.

Finally Jesus said to Peter, "Follow me!"

Jesus and John (John 21:20-24)

Peter turned around and saw John, the team member who'd always been a real mate to Jesus, walking behind them. It was John who'd sat next to Jesus at their last meal before his death, and said, "Lord, who is the traitor?"

Peter saw John and said, "What about this bloke, Lord—what'll happen to him?"

Jesus said, "That's not your concern. If I want him to live until I come back, what concern is that of yours? Your job is to follow me!"

That's why some people at the time went around saying that John wouldn't die. But Jesus didn't say that John wouldn't die. He just said, "If I want him to live..."

John is the eyewitness to these things—and he's known to be a truthful bloke.

The last word (John 21:25)

There are heaps of other things that Jesus did, and if all of them were written down, the whole planet would be drowning in books about Jesus!

Psalm 23

God is the Station Owner,
And I am just one of the sheep.
He musters me down to the lucerne flats,
And feeds me there all week.

When I'm feeling poorly,
And at something less than my peak,
He leads me to the restfulness,
Of a coolabah shaded creek.

He teaches me not to break away,
Not to be a loner;
He teaches me to stick with His mob,
And acknowledge Him as my Owner.

Even when the droughts are bad,
And I cross the Desert of Death,
God is close beside me,
So close I can feel His Breath.

God is the one who holds the map,
That gives me my direction,
And God is the one who guarantees,
Provision for my protection.

Although there are dingos in the hills,
And the paddocks are full of snakes,
God serves up a barbecue,
Of beautiful T-bone steaks!

His patience and compassion,
And forgiveness fail me never;
And I'll live with Him in the Homestead,
Beyond the end of forever.

Glossary

A

aggro – angry

argy-bargy – argument

all mouth and no trousers – an empty show, insincere, hypocritical

ankle biters – small children

ankle, to – to walk

artesian bore – a deep well

arvo – afternoon

as mad as a cut snake – angry

B

backblocks – out in the sticks, remote rural area

bananas – excited (can be either "excited happy" or "excited angry")

barbie – barbecue

beauty – good (a word of general approval)

big do, a – a big social event

big wigs – important people

billy – short for 'billy can' (container for boiling water on a campfire to make tea)

bingo! – instantly! at once! hit the jackpot!

blagger – robber

bloke – a guy, a man or boy

blow a fuse – become angry

blow me down – an expression of surprise

bonzer – good (a word of general approval)

boofhead – idiot

boss cocky – the one in charge

bottler – good (a word of general approval)

Broome – very remote city on the west coast of Australia

bub – a baby

budgie – a small bird

bun in the oven, having a – pregnant

bung on – to perform, to stage, to put on

bungalow – a house

bunny rug – a small, warm blanket to wrap a baby in (usually either pink or blue)

bush telegraph – the grape vine (general gossip or news)

bushrangers – outlaws, thieves operating on the open road

busy as a one armed paper hanger in a gale – very, very busy

C

cadger – beggar

cark – die

cat got your tongue? – why are you silent? can't you say something?

cheesed off – annoyed

chockers – full ('chock full')

chooks – hens, chickens

chuck – throw (or toss or pitch)

chuck a wobbly – panic

cobber – friend, mate

cockatoo – a large bird, common in the Australian bush

codger – an old person

colly wobbles – illness, sickness

cooee – a call heard in the Australian outback (to attract attention)

coolabah – a common Australian native tree

couldn't lie straight in bed – habitual liar

crack a keg – turn on the beer

creek – a small stream

cronies – friends, collaborators

crook – sick, ill, unwell

cuppa – a cup of tea

cyclone – hurricane

D

damper – a loaf of bread

dead – often used as an intensifier, so that it means "very" (e.g. "dead keen" means "very keen" and so on)

dead-set – for sure and certain

dingo – the Australian wild dog (the equivalent of the coyote)

do your lolly – become angry, get real mad

dough – money

drover – cowboy, rural worker (shifting herds of animals from one place to another)

drum, the – the news, the gossip

E

ear bash – talk, lecture ('given an ear bashing' means spoken to, or lectured)

egg-head – professor

excited as a race horse on Melbourne Cup day, as
– very excited (the Melbourne Cup is Australia's
biggest annual horse race: the equivalent of the
Kentucky Derby)

F

fair dinkum – genuine, reliable, dependable, honest

fiver, a – five dollars

flash – showy or ostentatious

flog – push, promote

footie – football

fuse, blow a – get angry

G

g'day – greeting (short for 'good day')

giving heaps – giving trouble, being aggressive
(often in the form of verbal abuse)

going bananas – becoming excited

goner – dead (or destroyed)

good oil – genuine or reliable news

grub – food

gully – a dip or depression in the ground, often a
dry water-course

H

happy as Larry – happy

head honchos – people in power

heaps – many, lots

homestead – farm house

humpy – a small shack, a modest dwelling

hunky dory – alright, okay, fine

I

illywacker – cheat, fraud, con man

J

jumpy as a wallaby on hot rocks, as – very
   nervous (a wallaby is a small kangaroo)

K

kick the kitty – contribute money
kip – sleep
knock back, to – to refuse, to reject
knock off – stop (can also mean "kill")
knock your socks off – astonish you
knocked them all for six – surprised them (from
   the game of cricket where a "six" is the equivalent
   of a home run)
knocked sideways – surprised

L

large as life and twice as ugly, as – something
   surprising but real
like a bandicoot on a burnt ridge – all alone
little nipper – small child, or baby
lucerne flats – well grassed paddocks

M

make tracks – travel
Mallee bull, a – a large, strong animal (anyone who
   is like a Mallee bull is very fit and strong)

mate – friend

merino – sheep

mob – crowd (or gang or flock or herd)

more degrees than an a thermometer – professors with lots of college degrees

mucking about – wasting time

mug – a gullible fool

mulga – the bush, the outback or countryside

mum – the way Australians spell (and pronounce) "mom"

N

nag (noun) – a horse

nag, to (verb) – to pester, to annoy, to keep on and on about something

nick off – depart (perhaps hurriedly)

nip off – depart (perhaps hurriedly)

noggin – head

nope – no

not on your Nellie! – not a chance!

O

old chap – used as an informal greeting

old duck – elderly woman

old man – often used to mean a woman's husband, or someone's father (or ancestor)

Old Nick – Satan

onya – expression of support and approval (short for 'good on you')

P

paddock – field
paspalum – native grass
pink, in the – healthy
popped the sprog – given birth
pop up – appear
preggers – pregnant
pressies – presents, gifts
pub – hotel (or motel)

Q

quid – money (a bill worth about two dollars)

R

railway sleepers – cross-ties (under railroad tracks)
rellies (or **rels**) – relatives
ridgy didge – genuine, real, accurate information
rough end of the stick – unkind or unfair treatment

S

scuttle – run, hurry
scrub – the bush, the countryside
sheila – woman or girl
shire – district
shot through like a Toorak tram – depart hurriedly,
    rushed away
shove off! – go away!
silo – building for storing harvested grain
sky pilot – priest or minister
smackers – money (usually bills)

snake in the grass – traitor

spot on – correct

sprog – child

squiz – an inquiring look

stack on a turn – become angry

staggered – surprised

starve the lizards – an expression of surprise

station owner – farmer, ranch owner

stone the crows – an expression of surprise

straight up – honestly, truly

stunned mullet – the look of someone who has been surprised, someone with an amazed and surprised look on their face

T

tea leaf – thief (rhyming slang)

teetotaller – non-drinker

telegraph pole – an old name for a power pole

thick as three short planks – stupid, slow on the uptake

tick off – lecture, tell off, reprimand

tickled – pleased

tickled pink – very pleased

tiddler – a very small fish

tinnie – a can of beer

toddler – a small child

toffee nose – a snob, a self important person

toffs – rich people

toodle-oo – goodbye

tout – a small time criminal

town bike – woman of low morals

tucker – food
tucker bag – food container
tumbled – understood
tumble off the twig – die
tyke – a small child

V
veranda – front porch

W
wallop – hit
weak at the knees – nervous, frightened
whinge – whine, complain
whiz – quickly, hurry
wowser – one who objects to low morals, or a
    morals crusader
wrinkly – old (an old person)

Y
yabbering – chatting, talking
yarn – a talk, a chat
yonks – a long time, years (usually in the sense of
    'many years')
you beaut! – terrific! (an expression of enthusiastic
    approval)

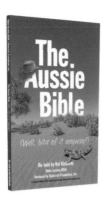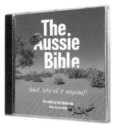

You can get a fair dinkum copy of The Aussie Bible in CD or book form at your local bookstore or on the net at www.theaussiebible.com

To contact the publisher or order bulk quantities
of The Aussie Bible, write to:

**Glencroix Promotions, Inc.
1928 Spring Garden Street, 2F
Philadelphia, Pennsylvania 19130-3859**

Notes

Notes

Notes

Notes